FÉNELON

Meditations
on the
Heart of God

BY FRANÇOIS FÉNELON

TRANSLATED BY
ROBERT J. EDMONSON

PARACLETE PRESS
Brewster, Massachusetts

Library of Congress Cataloging-in-Publication Data

    Fénelon, François de Salignac de La Mothe -, 1651-1715.
    [Fragments spirituels. English. Selections]
    Fénelon: Meditations on the Heart of God / by François Fénelon;
    translated and modernized by Robert J. Edmonson.
    p.cm.
    ISBN: 1-55725-181-9 (pbk.)
    1. Meditations. 2. God–Love–Meditations. 3. God–Worship and
    love–Meditations. 4. Spiritual life–Catholic Church. 5. Catholic
    Church–Doctrines. I. Edmonson, Robert J. II. Title. III. Title:
    Meditations on the heart of God.
    BX2183.F34213 1997
    231'.6–DC21   97-3487
                                   CIP

10 9 8 7 6 5 4 3 2

Published by Paraclete Press
Brewster, Massachusetts
Printed in the United States of America

Cover artwork credit: Erich Lessing / ArtResource, NY

Table of Contents

MEDITATIONS ON THE HEART OF GOD

Foreword

Why has Fénelon—a man who lost his job, his fame, his money and many of his friends—had such a wide readership for three centuries? Perhaps it is because surrounded by the splendor and decadence of the most powerful court in Europe, he chose a different path, one that took him through enormous inner suffering and into a relationship with God that few have known. His life reflected the truth of these words penned by Thomas à Kempis two centuries before him:

> Whosoever, therefore, with a single heart shall direct his attention upwards to God, and purify himself from all inordinate love or dislike of any created thing, shall be the most fit to receive grace, and worthy of the gift of devotion.—MATT. 6:22.

For the Lord bestows His blessing there where He finds the vessels empty.[1]

Having chosen this way, "the royal way of the cross," Fénelon became a shining example to men and women who sought his counsel. In English translation he is best known for the letters he wrote to his spiritual children. Though some of the original letters were lost, excerpts and copies of excerpts from many of them were handed around by the faithful for inspiration and eventually published. The present volume presents a number of these excerpts and short writings, all originally published in French in the early 1700s.

The word "heart" is used in this book to translate two words with different meanings. The one encountered most often is *le cœur*—the physical heart, used figuratively as the seat of the emotions. This is man's heart; it is that part of us that reaches out to God. The other is *le sein (de Dieu)*—God's bosom or heart. This word has a deeper meaning than any one English word can convey. In the high Middle Ages this expression was often used to mean "heaven." But in Fénelon's time it took on the additional meaning of "womb," the place where life begins and is nurtured. Thus the heart of God is the place the human heart seeks and longs for, the only place where our hearts will find rest.

Come with me now and sit at the feet of this beloved shepherd, and hear the words of a wise master whose gentle teachings were forged in the crucible of suffering. Let his words lead you through your places of suffering and brokenheartedness, into the heart of God.

RJE

Introduction

In 1651, when François Fénelon was born, an exhausted Europe was recovering from the Thirty Years' War. Britain could not provide a balance of power, embroiled as it was in the civil war that had led to the execution of its king in 1649. So the 1648 Peace of Westphalia had left France as the dominant power in Europe. Within France, a series of revolts against the crown had begun in 1648, and the outcome of the struggle was by no means certain.

France dominated in the arts and letters as well as in politics. The creation of the *Académie Française* (the French Academy) in 1635 had standardized the French language. In 1637 René Descartes had established the principles of modern science and philosophy. Throughout Europe, the French language, science and culture were held in such high esteem that the use of French was widespread in every court. The scene was set for the golden age of French literature.

It was into this moment of history that François Fénelon was born in southwestern France. Like so many of the ancient minor nobility, Fénelon's parents had a large family—and a long list of creditors. But their fervent loyalty to the crown during the revolts brought them letters of gratitude from the king. So when Fénelon chose to follow his uncle, the bishop of Sarlat, in pursuing a career in the church, his family's solid reputation had paved the way for his entry into higher studies. After being ordained and completing his doctorate in 1677, Fénelon soon began to minister, to preach—and to write.

During Fénelon's childhood, the young Louis XIV had firmly suppressed the disaffected nobles, and then contrived to keep the most powerful of them under his thumb by building the lavish palace of Versailles and enticing them to live there. He kept them busy with endless balls and theatrical and musical performances.

With the nobles firmly under his control, Louis turned his attention to another perceived threat to the unity of his realm. The Edict of Nantes (1598) had granted a measure of religious liberty to Protestants. After the death of Louis's queen in 1683 and his marriage to the devout Catholic Madame de Maintenon in 1684, Louis was not long in revoking the right of Protestants to practice their religion. Many fled the country—but those who stayed were required to convert to the Catholic faith.

Fénelon's talent having been quickly recognized, he was named soon after ordination as superior of a Paris mission to new converts to the Catholic church. By 1684 he was invited to preach in Meaux, whose bishop, Bossuet, was counted among France's finest orators. Soon Fénelon was invited to go on a preaching mission with the renowned prelate.

The revocation of the Edict of Nantes in 1685 created a need for the best Catholic preachers in France. The young Fénelon was named director of the mission to convert the Protestants of Saintonge and Aunis—the center of French Protestantism. There, Fénelon won the hearts of the Protestants with his gentleness and moderation. But Fénelon's restraint did not pass unnoticed among more extreme factions, who blocked his nomination as bishop of Poitiers.

His mission among the Protestants accomplished, Fénelon returned to Paris where he served as spiritual director to the duke and duchess of Beauvilliers and their family of eight daughters. Out of this experience came Fénelon's first major work. *The Education of Girls* revealed a remarkable presentation of the value of education for young women.

In 1689 the duke of Beauvilliers was named governor over the king's sons and grandsons. Having revealed his abilities as a teacher and preacher, Fénelon was immediately made personal tutor to the king's grandson, the young duke of Burgundy. By the age of 38 Fénelon had achieved a prominent platform for his gentle teachings.

For the benefit of his pupil, Fénelon wrote his *Fables* (moral lessons in the form of fairy tales), his *Dialogs of the Dead* (in which bygone historical figures tell what they learned from life), numerous spiritual writings, and *The Adventures of Telemachus* (a commentary in epic style on how kings ought to reign). For nearly ten years he devoted himself to his charge, patiently turning this wild young man into a model of docility.

As tutor to the heir to the throne, Fénelon gained access to the court of Versailles, where a group of devout Christians welcomed his presence and looked to him for guidance and spiritual direction. His friendship—and correspondence—with them continued throughout his life.

Among Fénelon's correspondents was Madame de Maintenon, who had founded a school for girls of impoverished nobility; Fénelon was a frequent visitor and speaker at the school.

The peak of Fénelon's career came in the mid-1690s, when he was elected to the *Académie Française* (1693) and appointed archbishop of Cambrai (1695). Another man would have lived out his life as a political favorite and died in comfortable obscurity. Fénelon, however, chose a different path. Surrounded by the untold wealth enjoyed by the courtiers at Versailles and by many members of the clergy, Fénelon sought a different treasure—a treasure that was to cost him the favor of Madame de Maintenon and the king, and his position at the court.

Before we attempt to understand Fénelon's fall from favor and subsequent banishment from the court, we must understand the era in which he lived.

The religious wars of the sixteenth century and the Thirty Years' War of the seventeenth century brought about widespread disillusionment with religious institutions. Alongside the religious fanaticism of these two centuries, a great flowering of art, music, literature and philosophy sprang up, as Renaissance humanism gave way to scientific rationalism.

Francis Bacon (1561-1626) denounced reliance on authority and Aristotelian logic, calling for a new scientific method based on inductive generalization from careful observation and experiment.

Galileo (1564-1642) created the science of mechanics and applied the principles of geometry to the motions of bodies.

Thomas Hobbes (1588-1679) later applied the principles of mechanics to every field of knowledge, emphasizing the law of self-preservation as the basis of human behavior.

But it was René Descartes (1596-1650) who had perhaps the most lasting influence on the French mentality. Refusing to accept any belief—even his own existence—until he could prove it to be necessarily true, he made mathematics the model for all science.

Not merely the province of an intellectual elite, these scientific and philosophical views permeated every level of French society, including the church. Their emphasis on the mind's reasoning left little room for the heart. One who sought to experience God with a deeper heart experience was viewed at best as anachronistic, and at worst as a dangerous threat to the strength of the nation.

There were a few whose experiences with God could not be ignored.

The French priest Saint Vincent de Paul (1581-1660) established charitable works to help society's most underprivileged.

The French nun Saint Margaret Mary Alacoque (1647-90) experienced visions of Christ.

The simple French monk known as Brother Lawrence (1620?-1691) determined to practice the presence of God throughout his life.[2]

In 1688 Fénelon met a woman whose teachings were to have a profound effect on his experience of God. Though steeped in the culture and teaching of his day, Fénelon felt a perplexing lack in his life that remained unfulfilled until his encounter with Madame Guyon.

Jeanne Guyon (1648-1717) had begun to introduce into France the doctrine of quietism, based on the belief that perfection lies in the utter abandonment of oneself to God. At first well received by the clergy and the pope, the doctrine soon aroused severe criticism because the abandonment it calls for can turn into passivity.

The archbishop of Paris was quick to criticize Madame Guyon, and in 1688 she was imprisoned. But she was released the next year through the influence of Madame de Maintenon, and during the next several years she was often present at the court, forming a circle of friends including Fénelon. Eventually, however, Madame de Maintenon began to find Madame Guyon's teaching suspect.

Without the aid of her former protectress, Madame Guyon was imprisoned again in 1695. This time her incarceration was to last until 1703, when she was released on the condition that she live in exile from Paris.

In 1695, the year of Madame Guyon's second imprisonment, Fénelon was made archbishop of Cambrai. Due to the entangled European politics of the time, his appointment carried not only religious authority, but several titles of nobility—and considerable revenues. And Fénelon was still tutor to the king's grandson. At the age of 44, this son of impoverished provincial minor nobility had achieved enormous prestige.

But 1695 marked a turning point in Fénelon's life, for in that year he became involved in a controversy with Bossuet over Madame Guyon's teachings. Having at last found satisfaction for his spiritual hunger, Fénelon felt the need to vindicate his spiritual mentor. But Bossuet, the celebrated orator who had once aided Fénelon's career, now aimed his acerbic pen at the one who rose to Madame Guyon's defense. Thomas Merton explains what happened:

Bossuet was a court preacher, a "solid" ecclesiastic, a man of duty, no doubt, and a great influence for good at Versailles. But he also knew the meaning of a career, and was too realistically engaged in the practicalities of that career to be bothered with the vicissitudes of interior conflict, or with the experience of trouble and of light which led Fénelon into the ways of the mystics. Dangerous ways, of course. One can well understand Bossuet's consternation at Fénelon's friendship with Mme Guyon. She was not only bizarre and rash, she was not only a distinctly bad influence among the devout ladies of Versailles, but some of her propositions were so strange as to seem heretical. This Bossuet could see. But because he saw this, he could see nothing else. He could not see that Fénelon saw it just as well. He could not see that Fénelon was able to distinguish between the error and the exaggeration of Mme Guyon's language, her neurotic excesses, and the core of genuineness in her experience. Nor did he realize that Fénelon had gone far beyond Mme Guyon, and had really understood the Catholic tradition of mysticism that led back through St Francis de Sales and St John of the Cross to the Fathers of the Church.[3]

The polemic between Fénelon and Bossuet continued for several years. When Fénelon published his *Explanation of the Maxims of the Saints* in 1697, the work was attacked by Bossuet as inconsistent with traditional Christian teachings. The two prelates appealed to Rome, and parts of the book were condemned by the pope in 1699.

Fénelon's statements were not always as safe as Bossuet's, and in one book [Maxims of the Saints] he set down a few formulas which, closely and technically examined, proved to be erroneous or ill-sounding. (Nothing of Fénelon's was ever found to be heretical.) The fact remains that in the realm of mysticism, Fénelon knew what he was talking about and Bossuet did not. Not only was Fénelon experienced in these matters, he was also the better, the more learned and wiser theologian. If the Church (the Pope himself being extremely reluctant) saw fit to censure some of the propositions in which Fénelon sought to refute quietism and correct its excesses, Rome has nevertheless repeatedly approved of the doctrine itself as it has been lived and taught by the saints. The most recent of these is Thérèse of Lisieux, whose "little way" is not only very close to Fénelon, but often echoes him practically word for word. There is no more quietism in Fénelon than there is in the "little way" or, for that matter, in St John of the Cross.[4]

In 1699, the same year Fénelon's spiritual writings were condemned, his *Telemachus* was published without his permission. Written for his royal pupil, the book for which Fénelon is best known in secular history states that kings exist for the benefit of their subjects, and denounces war. Louis XIV found the book to be an arrow aimed directly at his autocratic, war-filled reign. Fénelon was stripped of his position at court and exiled to his diocese.

Another man would have become bitter at such self-serving and cynical treatment. Fénelon's reaction to his condemnation and exile revealed the strength of his character. His defense of Madame Guyon had cost him everything he had worked so hard to achieve, but not a trace of bitterness could be found in him.

> Perhaps, after all, this gives us a clue as to the real "crime" of Fénelon in the eyes of the King and of the Court. He refused to submit to their power and he persisted in identifying himself with a cause that was, in their eyes, despicable chiefly because it was weak. This in turn is reflected in the judgment of later generations upon his spirituality. One could hardly do anything but ridicule a doctrine that seemed to put a premium on helplessness, passivity, and "annihilation." And this was a very convenient way of overlooking the real strength, indeed the *superior* moral strength, of Fénelon.[5]

True to the course he had set for himself, Fénelon submitted meekly to his condemnation and exile, and set about with considerable energy to improve the lot of the peasants of his diocese and deepen the spiritual life of all with whom he came in contact.

Right up until his death in 1715, Fénelon never ceased his correspondence with those at court who had become his spiritual children.

When Louis XIV's son died in 1711 and the young duke of Burgundy became the heir to the throne, the devout circles at court had great expectations. Had the young man ascended the throne and followed Fénelon's advice, who knows? Perhaps the horror of the French Revolution would have been avoided. But this was not to be, for the young man died before Louis XIV, and the king's spoiled and inept great-grandson took the throne as Louis XV.

To this day, French historians do not understand Fénelon. At best, he was the hapless upstart who dared to argue with Bossuet and condemn Louis XIV. At worst, he was a dangerous subversive who threatened the strength of the French nation.

But throughout Fénelon's lifetime and the centuries that have followed, Christians who have felt drawn toward a life of closer communion with God have found in Fénelon's writings a depth of understanding of their struggles that has been a source of profound encouragement. Fénelon's penetrating letters of advice and counsel to his friends have been translated and widely distributed in several languages.[6]

This volume of Fénelon's writings is presented with our prayer that it will bring you encouragement and strength on your journey toward the heart of God.

---

[1] *The Imitation of Christ*, chapter 15, section 3.

[2] *The Practice of the Presence of God* is available from the Paraclete Living Library.

[3] Thomas Merton, "Reflections on the Character and Genius of Fénelon," introduction to *Fénelon: Letters of Love and Counsel*, English translation © 1964 by the Harvill Press and Harcourt, Brace & World, Inc., pp. 11-12. Reproduced with permission from the Harvill Press.

[4] *Ibid*, p. 12.

[5] *Ibid*, p. 26.

[6] Other volumes of Fénelon's writings are available from the Paraclete Living Library.

About This Edition

The present volume is composed of excerpts taken from *Holy Reflections For Each Day Of the Month*, *Meditations On Various Subjects Taken From the Holy Scriptures*, and *Meditations For One Who Is Ill*, all published in the early 1700s.

Scripture references in this translation were taken for the most part from standard English versions. In some cases the French translation of the Latin Vulgate used by Fénelon differed enough from that of modern translations that a paraphrase of the Scripture reference is given to make his commentary clear. Some excerpts lacked Scripture verses and were left in their original form. However, in a few cases

Scriptures used within the text were placed at the beginning of the meditation.

Where excerpts had titles they were retained; titles suggested by the text were given to excerpts lacking them. Where the context indicated the need for emphasis, words were set in italics.

Finally, where concepts were used that would have been familiar in the eighteenth century but perhaps not in our time, or where Scripture verses or other quotations were used without a reference, explanatory footnotes were provided.

Acknowledgments

The task of rendering the late seventeenth-century French of the beloved author Fénelon into modern English must be undertaken with a grasp not only of the French language as it was used in that period, but of the author's life and thinking and the times that shaped them.

Much of the credit for this book must be given to LaVonne Neff, whose editing skills, command of French, and love of Fénelon's writings combined to produce insightful suggestions for improvement in its presentation and content.

Special thanks are also due to my wife Janet Edmonson for reading the manuscript and contributing valuable advice.

The encouragement of many friends helped Fénelon's words come to life. Special thanks are due to Lillian Miao,

Sarah Kanaga, Carolyn Clark, the Rev. Ronald Minor, and many others.

Finally, heartfelt thanks are owed to the staff of Paraclete Press, whose patience through this book's revisions is gratefully acknowledged.

one

Where Is Our Faith?

When the Son of Man comes, will he find faith on earth?
(Luke 18:8 RSV)

If the Son of Man were to come at this very moment, would he find faith in us? Where is our faith? Where is the evidence of it? Do we really believe that this life is only a short transition to a better one? Do we believe that we have to suffer with Jesus Christ before we spend eternity with him? Do we regard the world as a passing illusion, and death as the entrance into the treasures of real value?

Do we live by faith? Does it stir us to life? Do we cherish the timeless truths it presents us? Do we nourish our souls with faith, taking the same care to feed our souls that we take to nourish our bodies with proper food? Do we make it our practice to look at everything through the eyes of faith? Do we use our faith to correct all our thoughts and judgments?

Alas! Far from living by faith, we often cause faith to die in our minds and in our hearts. We think as if we were pagans, and we behave in the same way. If someone wanted to believe what he should believe, would he do what we do?

two

The Kingdom Within

Unless one is born of water and the Spirit, he cannot enter the kingdom of God. (John 3:5b RSV)

To see the kingdom of God which is inside us, we need to be born a second time and take on a new nature. Happy are those who have eyes to see that kingdom; flesh and blood are not capable of seeing it, because mere animal instinct is blind, and is content to be so.

To our fleshly nature, what God is doing inside us is only a dream. For us to see the wonders of that inner kingdom, we have to be reborn. And to be reborn, we have to die. Though the world may scorn, condemn, and mock us, to us it is given to believe, to accept, and to become fully alive.

When we take time for one simple moment of inner recollection and yielding ourselves to God, we see and hear more than the intellectual reasoning of all humanity put together. When we hush our desires and thoughts and turn our attention away from outward things, we enter into the light. And then it is that we discover God reigning on the throne of his kingdom—inside us.

three

The Narrow Door

Strive to enter by the narrow door. (Luke 13:24 RSV)

We can enter the kingdom of God only through hard struggle. We have to assault it as if we were laying siege to it. It has a narrow door. To get through that door, we have to put our sinful frames through discomfort by taking a low place, by submitting, by crawling, by making ourselves small.

The large, wide-open door that the crowd is passing through leads to destruction. All the wide roads that join together and lead to that wide-open door should make us feel afraid. In fact, when the world is laughing with us and our path seems sweet, we ought to realize how unfortunate we are! We will never be good for the life of eternity unless we feel ill at ease in this one.

So let us be careful not to follow the crowd that limits itself to following the broad and comfortable road. We must walk in the footsteps of that small band of saints, climbing up the steep-sloped path of repentance, clambering over the rocks with sweat on our faces. And we must expect that the last step in our lives will be yet one more violent effort to pass through the narrow door of eternity.

four

Molded Into Jesus' Image

I have been crucified with Christ. (Saint Paul, in Galatians 2:20a RSV)

Saint Paul is content to be crucified with Christ, because he knows that we have been predestined by God for one reason alone—to be molded into the image of his Son, being crucified with him on the cross. Just as he did, we must abandon every earthly pleasure; just as he was, we must remain constant in the midst of suffering.

How wretched we are—we want to tear ourselves away from that cross that joins us to our Master. We cannot abandon the cross without abandoning the crucified Jesus Christ. The cross and Jesus Christ cannot be separated.

So let us live and die with him. Let us not be afraid of

anything except failing to complete our sacrifice in patience and in love. Alas! All the efforts we make in this life serve only to bind us to the world and to tear us away from the cross.

five

Devotion To God (1)

If anyone thinks he is religious, and does not bridle his tongue but deceives his heart, this man's religion is vain. (James 1:26 RSV)

There are so many abuses that go under the name of religious piety! Some people's piety consists only in their many prayers. For others, piety consists in a great number of outward works done for the glory of God and the relief of their neighbors. Some consider piety to be a continual desire to gain their own salvation. Others think it consists in practicing great austerity.

All these things might be considered good; they are even necessary to a degree. But we would be wrong to think that true devotion to God consists merely in devout practices.

The devotion that makes us holy and devotes us entirely to God consists in doing all that God wants, and in accomplishing everything he desires from us, in every place and in every circumstance he places us.

Do as many kind gestures as you wish, do as many dazzling works as you please—but you will only be rewarded for doing the will of the sovereign Master. If the domestic who serves you did marvelous things in your home, but did not do the things you have asked him to do, you would not congratulate him for all those marvelous things he has done; you would be justified in complaining that he was serving you badly.

Perfect devotion requires us not only to do the will of God, but to do it with love. God loves for us to give to him joyfully. In everything he tells us to do, he always asks for our heart. Such a Master is worthy of our joyful service.

six

Devotion To God (2)

Our devotion to God must never stop. We must put it into practice everywhere—in things we do not like, in things that disturb us, in things that go against our point of view, our inclinations, our plans. True devotion holds us ready to give God everything—our well-being, our fortune, our time, our freedom, our life, and our reputation. To be willing to give of ourselves in this way, and to accept the consequences, is to be truly devout.

But since the will of God is often hidden from us, there is still one more step of renunciation and of death to self to be taken. It consists in accomplishing God's will through obedience—yes, blind obedience, but wise in its blindness. This is a condition that is required of every person. The most enlightened man or woman, the person who is the most gifted in calling others to God and the most capable of leading others to him, must also be led.

seven

God's Wisdom

The heavenly Father [will] give the Holy Spirit to those who ask him! (Luke 11:13b RSV)

There is no "holy spirit," no holy mind,[1] other than the mind and Spirit of God. Any mind or spirit that takes away from the only real treasure—no matter how penetrating, pleasant and capable that mind or spirit may be in gaining us corruptible treasures—is only a spirit of illusion that leads us astray. Would we want to ride in a magnificent and beautiful carriage that was only going to carry us over the edge of a cliff?

The mind and spirit are made for the sole purpose of leading to the truth and to sovereign good. Therefore there is no holy spirit, no holy mind, other than the Spirit of God—

because it is only his Spirit that leads us to him. So let us renounce our own minds, our own spirits, if we want to have God's. Happy are those who cast off their soiled clothing in order to put on the spotless garments that come from God. Happy are those who trample their empty wisdom under foot in order to embrace the wisdom that comes from the mind and Spirit of God!

[1] In French, the concepts rendered in English as "spirit" and "mind" are the same word: *esprit*. Here Fénelon moves freely from one concept to the other. To make the subtleties implied by the French text more understandable, both English words are placed here where appropriate.—*Tr.*

eight

A Holy Mind

Have this mind among yourselves, which is yours in Christ Jesus. (Philippians 2:5 RSV)

There is a great difference between a clever mind, a great mind and a holy mind. The clever mind is pleasing because of its charm. The great mind excites our admiration because of its depth. But only a right spirit can save and make us happy through its constancy and uprightness. Do not conform your ideas to those of the world. Distrust the mind as much as the world esteems it.

What we call "mind" is a certain facility for producing brilliant thoughts. But nothing is more vain. We make an idol of our minds, just as a woman who thinks herself beautiful makes an idol of her face. Our thoughts reflect who we are.

We must reject not only this false glitter of the mind, but also every trace of human wisdom, no matter how sincere and useful it may seem. Like little children, we must enter into simplicity of faith, into forthrightness and innocence, into dread of sin, into humiliation—and into the sacred folly of the cross.

nine

Patient Acceptance

In your patience possess ye your souls. *(Luke 21:19 KJV)*

The soul deserts its very nature when it becomes impatient. When it submits without complaint, it takes possession of itself in peace and comes into possession of God. To become impatient is to want what we do not have, and not to want what we do have. In so doing, the soul is handed over to its passions, and neither reasoning nor faith can hold it back, so troubled is it. Such weakness! Such swerving away from the right path!

As long as we desire the soul-sickness that brings us suffering—to us it is *not* sickness—why would we make our sickness a reality by ceasing to desire it?

Inner peace exists not in the flesh but in the will. We can

hold onto peace in the midst of the most violent suffering, as long as the will remains firm and submissive to God despite its abhorrence of the situation. Peace on this earth consists in *accepting* the things that are contrary to our desires, not in being exempted from suffering them, nor in being delivered from all temptations.

ten

What God Sends Is Right

Father, I have sinned against heaven and before you; I am no longer worthy to be called your son. (Luke 15:21, RSV)

To hear you bluster and complain, it would seem that you are the most innocent soul in the world, and that a crying injustice is being done to you not to let you back into the garden of Eden! Remember everything you have done against God, and acknowledge that he is right.

What you ought to do is tell God, with the same humility as the prodigal son, "'Father, I have sinned against heaven and before you.' I know what your justice demands of me, but I lack the courage to submit to it. If you were to place your confidence in me and spare me, I would become flattered, I would spare myself, and I would betray myself through that self-flattery. But your merciful hand performs what I would evidently never have had the courage to do. It strikes me out of kindness. Let me patiently bear those healing blows."

The least a sinner can do, if he is truly upset with himself, is to willingly bear the suffering that comes his way—suffering he would never have had the strength to choose.

eleven

Loving God's Will

Thy will be done, on earth as it is in heaven. (*Matthew 6:10b* RSV)

Nothing happens here on earth, just as nothing is done in heaven, except by God's will. But men do not always love the will of God. If we love God's will, and only God's will, we will turn earth into heaven. We will thank God for all he sends our way, the evil with the good; when he sends us afflictions, they become treasures.

We must not trouble ourselves about the past, because there is no evil that God has not allowed to befall a city,[2] that is, that he has not permitted and brought about in the order of his divine providence. And we must have no fear for the future, since nothing will happen to us unless God sends it or allows it.

21

O God, what do I see on every side, but your will that is being accomplished? Let it also be accomplished in me. Let me love it; let it make everything sweet. Let me bring my own will down to nothing. O God, may you be blessed for everything. Accomplish your will, Lord. It is yours to will, and mine to give myself over completely.

[2] Cf. Amos 3:6.

twelve

Jesus Our Model

I always do what is pleasing to him [the Father]. (John 8:29 RSV)

Dear Jesus, help us understand where this example ought to be leading us. Here is our model: you acted only according to the good pleasure of your Father—who is willing to be named our Father as well. Act in us as you yourself did—according to the Father's good pleasure. Let us be united inseparably to you, consulting only your plans and purposes.

It is not enough for us to pray, to teach others, to suffer, and to edify others. No, we must eat, sleep, and carry on conversations, having in mind only obedience to God's will. Then we will be in a state of continual sacrifice, uninterrupted love, unceasing prayer.

When, O Lord, will we reach that point? But it is up to you to apportion your gifts, and it is up to us to bring ourselves to nothing in your sight. Lord, do with us, not only outwardly, but deep within us, as it seems good to you. It is not for us to take the measure of your mercies.

thirteen

Concerning Prayer

But let him ask in faith, with no doubting, for he who doubts is like a wave of the sea that is driven and tossed by the wind. (James 1:6, RSV)

We are so dependent on God that not only *should* we do everything for him, but we are *unable* do anything except by him and for him. Therefore we ought to be asking God to give us the means to please him. And this happy necessity to run to him for all our needs, far from being a source of bother to us, ought to be the source of our complete consolation. What a blessing it is to speak to him in trust, to open our hearts to him, and by means of prayer to be united with him as much as it is possible to be in this life!

As Saint Cyprian said,[3] let us consider whether he will

25

grant us the good things he invites us to ask him for.[4] So let us pray faithfully, never losing the fruit of our prayers by wavering or hesitating in our faith, as Saint James says. Happy is the soul that gains comfort in prayer through the presence of its Beloved!

But how unhappy we are when all we feel is weariness at the heavenly pursuit we call "prayer." The lukewarmness of our prayers is the source of all our other unfaithfulnesses. So let us remember the words of Saint James—if anyone among us is in trouble, he should pray to obtain comfort.[5]

---

[3] The reference is to St. Cyprian's treatise on the Lord's Prayer.
[4] The conclusion is clear: certainly he will.
[5] James 5:13.

fourteen

Never Stop Knocking

Ask, and it will be given you; seek, and you will find; knock, and it will be opened to you. (Luke 11:9 RSV)

If all we had to do to obtain worldly riches was ask for them, we would be so eager, untiring, and persevering in our asking! If all we had to do to find treasure was dig for it, how much earth would we not move! If all we had to do to enter the king's private council and assume the highest position of honor was knock, such redoubled knocking would be heard!

But what do we not do to find blessing and happiness where they cannot be found? How many rebuffs, how many setbacks are we willing to endure for the phantom of worldly glory! How much suffering for vain pleasures of which nothing remains but remorse!

The treasures of God's grace are the only true riches—yet they are the only riches we balk at asking for and expecting.

However, we must never stop knocking! The promises of Jesus Christ are always faithful—it is we who are unfaithful in asking for them.

fifteen

Listen To The Right Voice

Lord, to whom shall we go? You have the words of eternal life. (Saint Peter, in John 6:68 RSV)

Jesus Christ is the One we must listen to. As far as people are concerned, we ought to listen to them and believe them only insomuch as they are full of Jesus Christ's truth and authority. Books are good only to the extent that they teach us the good news of the gospel. Therefore, let us go straight to that sacred source.[6]

Jesus Christ spoke and acted only so that we might listen to him and attentively study the details of his life. But how foolish we are! We run after our own thoughts, which are only vain and fruitless, and we neglect the truth himself, whose words are able to make us live forever.

Speak, O divine Word, O uncreated Word who took on human flesh for me! Let my soul hear you. Say everything you desire—I want everything that is pleasing to you.

[6] Or, *spring*. This passage invites us study the gospels.

sixteen

Doing God's Will

Do this, and you will live. *(Jesus Christ, in Luke 10:28b RSV)*

We often say we would like to know what to do to advance in virtue—but when the Spirit of God shows us what to do, we often lack the courage to carry it out.

We have a strong feeling that we are not what we ought to be. We see how our burdens grow day by day. Yet we feel we are doing a lot just by *saying* we want to be delivered out of ourselves. Let us count it as nothing if we say we are willing to follow God, and then do not go as far as *sacrificing* the things that stop us from walking in God's ways. Let us not hold the truth captive through our unrighteous half-heartedness.

So let us listen to what God inspires in us. Let us test the spirit that is moving in us, to see if it comes from God. And after we have recognized God, let us stop at nothing to make him happy. The psalmist does not simply ask God to teach him *what* his will is—he asks God to teach him to *do* it.[7]

[7] Psalm 143:10.

seventeen

The Right Use Of Crosses

The more we fear crosses, the more we have to conclude that we need them. And the heavier our crosses are, the more we have to believe that God loves us. We ought to judge the seriousness of our illnesses by the strength of the treatment the spiritual Physician applies to them.

We must be very corrupt, and God must be very merciful, since he takes great pains to heal us—even though the process of healing may be difficult. So let us turn our crosses themselves into a source of love, comfort and faith, saying with Saint Paul, "For this slight momentary affliction is preparing for us an eternal weight of glory beyond all comparison."[8]

Happy are those who go forth weeping, bearing the seed for sowing, for they will bring in an indescribably joyful harvest of eternal life![9]

[8] 2 Corinthians 4:17, RSV.
[9] Cf. Psalm 126:6.

eighteen

The Blessing Of Suffering

I have been crucified with Christ. (Saint Paul, in *Galatians* 2:20a RSV)

With the Savior we are bound to the cross, and it is he who binds us to it through his grace. It is because of Jesus that we do not want to leave the cross, because he cannot be separated from it. O holy and suffering body of Jesus, with which our bodies become united and form but one single victim, as you give me your cross, give me your spirit of death to self and abandonment.

Cause me to think less about my suffering than about the blessing of suffering with you. What am I suffering that you have not suffered? Or rather, how much have I suffered, if I dare compare myself to you?

O cowardly nature of mine, be silent. Look at your Master and blush with shame.

Lord, make me love and I will no longer be afraid of suffering. And then, if I do suffer difficult things that are painful to my nature, at least I will not be suffering any more than I am willing to suffer.

nineteen

Be Merciful

Be merciful, even as your Father is merciful. (Luke 6:36
RSV)

Just because other people are weak, is that a good reason to
speak more harshly to them? You who complain that others
are making you suffer, do you think you are not making anyone else suffer? You who are so shocked by your neighbor's
faults, do you imagine you are perfect yourself?

How dumbfounded you would be if all the people on
whom you keep pressing so hard were suddenly to turn
around and start pressing hard on you! But when you find
your justification on earth, could not God, who knows
everything, and who has many things he could reproach you
for—could he not silence you with a single word and stop

37

you? Does it not ever enter your mind to be afraid that he will ask why you do not show your brother a little of that mercy that he, who is your Master, showers so abundantly on you?

twenty

One Thing Is Needful

Martha, Martha! You are anxious and troubled about many things; one thing is needful. (Luke 10:41-42 RSV)

We think there are a thousand things we should be concerned with, but there is actually only one. If we take care of that one thing, all the others will find themselves done. And if we fail to take care of the one thing that is needful, all the others—no matter how successfully we may seem to do them—will fall into ruin. So why are we so torn between matters of the heart and our worldly cares?

From this day forward I resolve to give my total attention to the only thing on earth I ought to be concerned with. Illumined by God's holy light, I resolve to stop worrying and to do every moment, with all the strength of my mind and body, whatever God in his providence places in my path. I will not be grieved about turning everything else over to God, because it is not my work I am doing, but God's. And I ought to want to do only what God gives me to do.

I resolve not to become keenly excited about anything, because it is dangerous to want to appropriate God's work to ourselves. If we do that, then we do God's work in our own strength; we turn good into bad and we allow pride to take over. And then we become flushed with the pursuit of success. We conceal our illusion by using the pretext of seeking God's glory.

O God, give me the grace to be faithful in my actions, but indifferent to success. The only thing I ought to be concerned with is to desire your will and to quietly meditate on you—even in the midst of busy times. It is up to you to crown my feeble actions with such fruit as is pleasing to you—and none at all, if that is what you find best for me.

twenty-one

Be Ready

You must also be ready; for the Son of man is coming at an unexpected hour. (Luke 12:40 RSV)

These words of Jesus were said to every person, without exception. They are accomplished in every person of good will, even though we may have made preparation for death. We make plans that presuppose we will live a long life, whereas life is going to end. The time people do not think will be their last often actually is. Perhaps death will come at this time in our lives. If people who are nearing the end of an incurable illness still hold onto hope for healing, how much more hope do we hold onto when we are in the fullness of health!

But where does this stubborn hope in life come from? It comes from the fact that we love life with a passion. And where does our strong desire to keep death away come from? It comes from the fact that we do not love the kingdom of God or the splendor and majesty of the life to come.

O men who are slow of heart, who cannot rise above this earth where we are so forlorn! The true way to hold ourselves at the ready for our last moment is to care little for all other moments, and always to live in expectation of our life's end.

twenty-two

Steadfastness In Hope

Eye hath not seen, nor ear heard, neither have entered into the heart of man, the things which God hath prepared for them that love him. (1 Corinthians 2:9 KJV)

What relationship is there between what we do here on earth, and what we hope for in heaven? The first Christians never stopped rejoicing at the sight of what they were hoping for—for at every moment, they believed they were seeing heaven open before them. Suffering, disrepute, torture, cruel deaths—none of these things had the power to dishearten them. They were intimately acquainted with God's infinite generosity in rewarding such sufferings—and they never thought they suffered enough. They were transported by joy when they were judged worthy of some deep humiliation.

And what about us? Fainthearted souls that we are, we know nothing about suffering, because we do not know how to hope. We become overwhelmed by the slightest crosses—often even those we bring on ourselves because of our own pride, rashness, and weakness!

twenty-three

A Harvest Of Joy

*May those who sow in tears reap with shouts of joy!
(Psalm 126:5 TEV)*

We have to sow seed in order to gather a harvest. This life
is intended for sowing. In the next life we will enjoy the
fruits of our labors. But we earthbound men and women are
so fainthearted and impatient—we want to reap before we
sow. We want God to comfort us and make the way smooth
in order to lead us to himself. We express a desire to serve
him, provided that our service to God costs us little. Our
arrogance leads us to hope for a great many things, but we
want to suffer very few things.

How blind we are! Will we never see that the kingdom of
Heaven is taken by violent attacks, and that only souls who

violently and courageously gain victory over themselves are worthy of winning Heaven?[10]

So let us weep here on earth. For happy are those who weep now,[11] but how terrible it will be for those who laugh now.[12] How terrible for those who have their consolation in this world! The time will come when those vain joys will be put to confusion. Then the world will have its turn to weep. And God himself will wipe away all tears from our eyes.[13]

[10] Matthew 11:12.
[11] Matthew 6:21.
[12] Luke 6:25.
[13] Revelation 21:4.

twenty-four

Our Daily Bread

Give us each day our daily bread. (Luke 11:3, RSV)

O God, what is this bread? It is not only the physical sustenance that in your providence you give us for the necessities of life, but it is also the nourishment of *truth* that you give daily to our souls. That kind of bread nourishes us unto eternal life. It makes our souls grow and become robust when our faith is tested. Every day, you renew this bread. Both inwardly and outwardly, you give our souls precisely what we need to continue in our life of faith and self-denial.

All I have to do is to eat this bread, and in a spirit of sacrifice to receive all the bitter-tasting things that you send my way—both in outward matters and in the depths of my heart.

Indeed, *what happens to me in the course of each day* is *my daily bread*—provided I do not refuse to take it from your hand and feed on it.

twenty-five

Hunger For Righteousness

Blessed are those who hunger and thirst for righteousness, for they shall be satisfied. (Matthew 5:6 RSV)

Why do we not have this hunger and thirst? Why are our souls not as hungry and thirsty as our bodies are? Bodies that have no desire for food are sick. In the same way, our souls suffer from sickness when we do not seek after the things that satisfy them, nor the food and drink that come from God.

The soul's food is truth and righteousness. To know good, to be filled with it, to strengthen ourselves with it— this is the spiritual food, the food from Heaven, that we need to eat. So let us reach out and eat it; let us be hungry for it. Let us stand before God as poor beggars who wait hopefully and expectantly for a little bread. Let us be aware of our weakness and our failure. How terrible for us if we forget how weak we are!

Let us read, let us pray, with that hunger to nourish our souls and that burning desire to quench our thirst. Only a continual great desire to be taught by God can make us worthy of discovering the wonders of his law.

Each of us receives this sacred bread to the extent that we desire it.

twenty-six

True Peace

Peace I leave with you; my peace I give to you; not as the world gives do I give to you. (John 14:27 RSV)

Every one of us is searching for peace, but we do not always search for it where it can be found. The peace that the world hopes for is as different and as removed from the peace that comes from God, as God himself is different and removed from the world. To put it another way, the world promises peace, but it *never* gives it. The world does offer a few passing pleasures—but those pleasures cost far more than they are worth.

Jesus alone can give peace to mankind. He brings us into harmony with himself. He brings our passions into submission. He sets limits to our desires. He comforts us through the hope of riches that will never perish. He gives us the joy of the Holy Spirit and causes us to taste that inner joy even when we are suffering. The spring that produces peace cannot run dry, and the depths of the soul in which it resides cannot be reached by all of humanity's evil; therefore for the righteous person it becomes a treasure that no one can take away.

True peace can be found only in possessing God. And possessing God here in this life can be found only in submission to faith and obedience to God's law. Both of these things reflect a pure and unalloyed love in the depths of the heart.

Therefore, thrust away all forbidden things. Cut out all unlawful desires. Dismiss all your bustling about and your worrying. Desire only God, seek only God, and you will enjoy peace—in spite of the world. What is troubling you? Poverty? Ridicule? Failure? Inward and outward crosses? Look on all these things as genuine favors from the hand of God, distributed to his friends, favors that he allows you to share. Then the world will change complexion, and nothing will take away your peace.

twenty-seven

True Joy

I looked upon laughter as a dream, and I said to joy, "Why do you deceive me?" (Ecclesiastes 2:2, according to the Vulgate).

The world rejoices as do sick persons who are in the throes of delirium or as do sleepers who have pleasant dreams. People thrash about, but only in vain—because they are committed to a hollow image, a passing figure, a fleeting shadow. When we are in that state we rejoice, but only because we are deceiving ourselves into believing we possess many things—when actually we do not possess anything at all.

If we have sought after the world's joy, when we awake from death we will find ourselves empty-handed. And then how ashamed we will be of our joy! How terrible therefore for people who find false comfort in this world that will exclude them from true comfort! So let us never stop saying to the vain and fleeting joy inspired by this world, "Why do you deceive me so rudely?"

Nothing is worthy of giving us joy except our blessed hope. Everything else, because it is not founded on that hope, is only a dream.

twenty-eight

Seek The Water That Satisfies

Everyone who drinks of this water will thirst again. (John
4:13 RSV)

The more we drink the impure and poisoned waters of
this age, the thirstier we are for them, and the more we
plunge into the world. Desires come to life in our hearts. The
possessions that come through riches only excite our greed,
for ambition is more unhappy because of what it does not
have, than satisfied with all it does possess.

Enjoying the world's pleasures only makes the soul thirsty
and weak. The soul becomes corrupted; it can never be satisfied. The more a person lets himself go, the more he wants
to succumb.

It is easier to keep our heart in a state of repentance and

burning desire for God than to bring it back to him once it has gone down the slope of pleasure and laxity.

So let us keep watch over ourselves. Let us stay away from drinking water that only increases our thirst. Let us keep careful watch over our hearts, for fear that the world and its vain comforts will come in and trouble our peace.

twenty-nine

Happy Tears

Blessed are those who mourn, for they shall be comforted.
(Matthew 5:4 RSV)

Such a new kind of tears, said Saint Augustine—they make
the people who shed them become happy. Their happiness
comes from being afflicted and grieving over the corruption
of the world around us, the world's pitfalls that surround and
try to trap us, and the wickedness we see within our own
hearts.

It is a great gift from God to be afraid of losing his love
and to be afraid of straying from the narrow path. It is the
one good possession in this life. When we are in danger of
losing everything we have and of losing even our own selves,
we should not be full of joy. When all we see in ourselves is

vanity, backsliding, scandal, forgetfulness of and defiance toward God whom we love, we grieve.

So let us weep when we see others and ourselves in God's holy light; let us weep—our sadness will gladden God's heart. He himself is the One who inspires that sadness in us. It is his love that makes our tears flow. Then we will become happy—because God himself will come and wipe away our tears.

thirty

Eternal Riches

We hear Jesus say, "Woe to you that laugh now"[14]—and yet we want to laugh. We hear him say, "Woe to you that are rich, for you have received your consolation"[15]—and yet we are constantly seeking after earthly riches. He says, "Blessed are you that weep now"[16]—and yet the thing we are most afraid of is to weep.

Here on this earth it is true that we ought to be weeping, not only for the dangers of our sinful condition, but for everything around us that is vain and dissolute. Let us weep for ourselves, and for those around us. Everything we see both inside ourselves and outside ourselves is only affliction of spirit, temptation and sin. Everywhere we find cause for tears. How truly terrible it is to love the things that are so unworthy of being loved. Now *that* is a reason for weeping! Shedding tears is the best thing we can do.

Happy are the tears that are brought about by grace, causing us to lose our desire for things that will pass away, and giving birth within us to the desire for riches that will never perish!

[14] Luke 6:25.
[15] Luke 6:24.
[16] Luke 6:21.

thirty-one

Earthly Wisdom

To set the mind on the flesh is death. (Rom. 8:6a RSV)

Worldly people have shrewd and wise minds, as Jesus tells us in the gospel—and their wisdom is often greater than that of godly people. But in spite of its dazzling, deceptively beautiful appearance, worldly wisdom has a fearsome flaw—*it brings death to all who take it as the rule by which they live.* Tortuous in its logic and abounding with subtleties, worldly wisdom is the enemy of God's wisdom, for God always walks in uprightness and simplicity. What good are all their talents to those who are worldly-wise, since they find themselves caught in their own traps?

Saint James the apostle says such wisdom is earthly, unspiritual and devilish.[17] It is earthly because it limits its concern to acquiring and owning earthly goods. It is unspiritual because it aspires only to furnish others with what fires their passions and to plunge them into sensual pleasures. It is devilish because, in addition to having the mind, spirit and shrewdness of the devil, it has all his evil intent.

With earthly wisdom, we imagine we are deceiving others—when actually we are deceiving only ourselves.

[17] James 3:15.

thirty-two

Trust God

It is better to take refuge in the Lord than to put confidence in man. (Psalm 118:8 RSV)

Every day you put your trust in friends who are weak, in people who are unknown to you, in unfaithful household servants. And yet you are afraid of trusting God! The signature of a public official puts your mind at ease about your possessions, yet the everlasting good news of Jesus Christ does not give you any reassurance at all! The world makes you every sort of promise, and you believe it. But God swears his promises to you, and you find it hard to believe him. How shameful this is for him! What a terrible thing this is for you!

Let us put things back in their proper order. With temperance and moderation let us do the things that depend on us.

Let us faithfully await the things that depend on God. Let us control any unchecked emotions, any anxiety disguised as right thinking or zeal.

Those who live in such a way establish their foundation on God, and become immovable like Mount Zion.

thirty-three

Strength Through Weakness

When I am weak, then I am strong. *(2 Corinthians 12:10 RSV)*

Lord, when I thought I could do everything, I could do nothing. And now that it seems to me I can no longer do anything, I am beginning to be able to do everything in you who strengthens me.[18] How blessed is my lack of ability, because it makes me find in you everything that is lacking in me! I rejoice in my weakness, because it opens my eyes to what the world is—and to what I really am in myself. I count it a blessing to be laid low by your hand, because it is in your making me into nothing that I will be covered by your almighty power.

Some people feel pity for me because I have been brought

low. You are blind, my friends! Do not feel sorry for this person who is loved by God, and on whom he brings suffering only out of love. It was in the past that I was to be pitied, when corrupt prosperity was poisoning my heart, and I was so far from God.

[18] Philippians 4:13.

thirty-four

On God's Mercy

The Lord is gracious and merciful, slow to anger and abounding in steadfast love. (Psalm 145:8 RSV)

As you stand before God, think about the mercy he has shown you, the enlightenment he has given you, the good thoughts he has inspired in you, the pitfalls of this world from which he has kept you safe, and the way he has helped you inwardly. Allow yourself to be moved to tears as you remember all the precious signs of his goodness.

Think about the crosses he has entrusted to you so that you may become a living sacrifice, because they are the clear signs of his love. Let your gratefulness for the past inspire you with trust for the future. Be persuaded that he has loved you too much not to love you still.

Do not mistrust God—no, you must mistrust yourself. Remember that he is, as Saint Paul put it, "the Father of mercies and God of all comfort."[19] Ask him, with King David, "Lord, where is thy steadfast love of old?"[20]

God has taken away the soft and comfortable things from your life. Why? Because you need to be humbled and to come to know yourself; because in vain you have sought elsewhere for help and comfort.

[19] 2 Corinthians 1:3, RSV.
[20] Psalm 89:49 RSV.

thirty-five

On Becoming Mature

Lord, what wilt thou have me to do? *(St. Paul, in Acts 9:6 KJV)*

Saint Paul was miraculously turned around and changed by the grace of the Savior he was persecuting. Alas! How much have we persecuted him through our unfaithfulness, our petulance, our untamed emotions that have disturbed the work he is doing? He has had to bring us low through trials; he has had to crush our pride; he has had to baffle our fleshly wisdom; he has had to dismay our vaunted self-worth.

Therefore let us say to him, "Lord, what wilt thou have me to do?—I am ready to do anything you ask." We must make this offer complete, holding nothing back. We must not make vague promises we will not actually put into practice when it comes to details. Saint Augustine tells us that for too long we have been dragging around with weak wills, longing after good but not putting forth the effort to bring it about.

It does not cost us anything to *want* to become mature, if we do not put forth any *effort* to become mature. We need to want God's maturity and perfection in our lives more than anything else.

So let us each probe our hearts and ask ourselves—am I determined to sacrifice to God my strongest friendships, my most deeply rooted habits, my foremost inclinations, my most gratifying pleasures?

thirty-six

Time Is Precious

Let us do good while we still have time. (Galatians 6:10, according to the Vulgate)
Night comes when no one can work. (John 9:4b RSV)

Time is precious, but we do not know yet how precious it really is. We will only know when we are no longer able to take advantage of it. Our friends ask for our time as if it were nothing, and we give it as if it were nothing. Often our time is our own responsibility; we do not know what to do with it, and we become overwhelmed as a result. The day will come when a quarter-hour will seem more valuable and desirable than all the fortunes in the universe.

Liberal and generous in every way, God in the wise economy of his providence teaches us how we should be prudent about the proper use of time. He never gives us two moments at the same time. He never gives us a second moment without taking away the first. And he never grants us that second moment without holding the third one in his hand, leaving us completely uncertain as to whether we will have it. Time is given to us to prepare for eternity. Eternity will not be long enough for us to ever stop regretting it if on this earth we have wasted time.

thirty-seven

On The Use Of Time

See, then, that ye walk circumspectly, not as fools but as wise, redeeming the time, because the days are evil. (Ephesians 5:15-16 KJV)

All our heart and all our time are not too much to give to God; he gave them to us only to serve and love him. So let us not hold anything back from him. We cannot be doing great things all the time, but we *can* do the things that are suitable to our condition in life. We are already doing a great deal if we hold our tongues, suffer, and pray when we cannot do something outwardly.

To offer up to God each mishap, setback, complaint, or confusion. To comfort a sick person, encourage a downcast soul, prevent suffering at its onset, teach a person who needs instruction, or soften the heart of someone who is bitter—all these things serve to redeem eternity through the good use of time.

But to truly gain eternity, we must redeem the time itself, as Saint Paul says. This means we must renounce engaging in excessive amusements and unnecessary exchanges with other people. We need to renounce pouring out our hearts to others in order to flatter our self-esteem and carrying on conversations that divert the mind, so we can be free to go about God's work more diligently. Promise him that you will be faithful to your disciplines of prayer and worship.

thirty-eight

The Radiant Path Of Faith

Walk before me, and be thou perfect. (Genesis 17:1b KJV)

Lord, this is what you said to faithful Abraham, and in fact everyone who walks in your presence has true perfection. We lose our perfection only when we lose sight of you. When we keep our eyes unceasingly turned toward you, we have everything. Alas! Where am I going when I do not see you at all? Where is my purpose? What is it? Where is my light? If we keep our eyes fixed on you with every step we take, we will never stray for a moment. How wonderful it is to remain on the radiant path of faith!

O shining faith! O admiring gaze that brings man to maturity and completion! O God!—wherever I look, it is you alone that I see in everything that my eyes seem to behold. Your providence is what holds my attention. My heart keeps watch only for you in the midst of the multitude of business affairs, duties and even thoughts that you oblige me to have. I center all my concentration on you, the sovereign and sole object of my attention.

To divide my thoughts in order to obey you is to reunite them with your will. What could I see in unworthy created things if you ceased to ask me to apply myself to them, and if I ceased to see you through them?

thirty-nine

God's Kindly Hand (1)

Yea, I have loved thee with an everlasting love; therefore, with loving-kindness have I drawn thee. (Jeremiah 31:3b KJV)

God did not wait for us to become something before he would love us. No, before the worlds came into being, and even before we had our very existence, he was thinking about us. And his desires for us were only to do us good.

What he once meditated on in eternity, he has carried out in time. His kindly hand has showered us with every sort of good thing. And even though our expressions of unfaithfulness and ingratitude almost equal the instances of his favors toward us, they have never been able to stop the flow of his gifts or dam up the flood of his graces.

O love without measure, you have made me what I am, you have given me what I have, and you promise me infinitely more besides! O love that has no beginning, you have loved me for infinite ages, even when I could neither feel nor recognize your love! O love that knows no interruption or inconstancy, love that all the bitter waters of my iniquities have never been able to extinguish! Have I a heart, O my God, if I am not completely filled with gratitude and tenderness toward you?

forty

God's Kindly Hand (2)

If anyone does not love the Lord, let him be outcast. Maranatha—Come, O Lord! (1 Corinthians 16:22 NEB)

What do I see? A God who, even after having given absolutely everything, gives himself. A God who comes to search for me even in the darkest depths because my sin has made me descend that far. A God who takes the form of a slave in order to deliver me from being enslaved by my enemies. A God who makes himself poor in order to make me rich. A God who calls me and runs after me when I flee from him. A God who dies in torment to snatch me from the arms of death and to give me back a life of blessing. And yet how often do I want neither him nor the life he is offering me!

What kind of person could love another person as God

loves us? Of how much would we be worthy of being out-cast if after all God has done, we did not love the Lord Jesus!

forty-one

True Love For God

Whom have I in heaven but thee? And there is nothing upon earth that I desire besides thee. (Psalm 73:25 RSV)

When we tell God we love him with all our heart, often we are just using words, making a speech that has no reality. From our childhood on, many of us have been taught to speak in such a way, and so we continue to do so when we have grown up—often without knowing what we are saying.

But to love God means to have no will other than his. It means faithfully to observe his holy law. It means to have a horror of sin. To love God means to love what Jesus loved—poverty, humiliation, suffering. It means to hate what Jesus hated—the world, our pride, our passions.

Could we think we love someone we would not want to

be like? To love God means to willingly have fellowship with him. It means to want to go to him in prayer. It means to sigh after and long for him. How false is a love that takes no pains to go and see One it loves!

forty-two

Divine Fire

I came to cast fire upon the earth, and would that it were already kindled! (Jesus, in Luke 12:49 RSV)

The fire that Jesus came to cast upon the earth is the fire of divine love. Jesus brought this fire to us in his heart, and now his only desire is to inflame our hearts with it as well. But men live in deadly coldness. We love a bit of money; we love land and houses. We love a reputation, a name, titles and credentials. We love to seek after changing, deadly things—such as conversations and pleasures that leave us empty afterwards. God is the only one for whom we have no more room for love. Instead, we exhaust ourselves running after the most wretched of his creations.

Jesus came to earth wanting nothing greater than to light

his divine fire in our hearts and make us feel the happiness and blessing of divine love. Yet we prefer the unhappiness of loving the lowest and most harmful things.

O God, reign over us in spite of our passions! How could we find anything to love outside of you? May the fire of your love extinguish any other fire! Give us the grace to love you, and we will love you and no other. And we will continue to love you throughout eternity.

forty-three

Set Me Apart

Though heart and body fail, yet God is my possession for-ever. (Psalm 73:26 NEB)

Is it possible to know you, dear God, and not love you? Your beauty, strength, grandeur, power and goodness; your generosity, magnificence and perfection of every kind, are far beyond what any created being could under-stand. And what touches me in the depths of my heart is that you love *me*. It might seem that the reverence I owe you and the vast inequality that exists between me and you ought to stop me from daring to love you. But you allow me—no, that is saying too little—you *command* me to love you. And so, Lord, I give up trying to know or own myself.

O sacred Love, you have wounded my heart, and yet you of your own free will were yourself wounded for me. So come now and heal me—or rather, come, take the wound you have given me and make it deeper and sharper. Set me apart from everything created. No longer can I be content with created things; they hinder me, they disturb me. You alone are sufficient for me; no longer do I desire anything but you.

forty-four

Set Me Aflame

What a wonder! Earthly lovers carry their foolish passions to extremes of fervent love—yet we who claim to love you do so weakly and faintheartedly. No, no, dear God, worldly love must not be stronger than divine love. Show what you can do with a heart that is completely given over to you.

My heart is open to you; you know its innermost recesses. You know what your grace has the power to stir up in it. You are only waiting for me to consent and give you my free will. This I do most ardently, a thousand times over!

Take possession of everything in me. Show yourself to be God. Set me aflame; consume me. Weak and powerless creature that I am, all that I have to give you is my love. Increase it, Lord, and make it more worthy of you. Oh, if only I were capable of doing great things for you! Oh, if only I had much to sacrifice for you! But all that I am capable of is so little. From this moment on all I want to do is sigh after you, long for you, and die to myself so that I may love you more.

forty-five

The Words Of Eternal Life

Lord, to whom shall we go? You have the words of eter-
nal life. (John 6:68 RSV)

We do not know the gospel well enough—and what pre-
vents us from learning that Good News is that we think we
already know it. But we are not acquainted enough with its
teachings and we do not enter into its spirit.

With great curiosity we search out the thoughts of men,
and yet we neglect the thoughts of God. One word of the
good news of the gospel is more precious than all the other
books in the world put together—it is the source of all
truth.

We ought to listen with such love, such faith, such adora-
tion, to the words of Jesus Christ in the gospel! From this

89

moment forward let us say to him, along with Saint Peter, "Lord, to whom shall we go? You have the words of eternal life."

forty-six

Let The Light Shine Through

Therefore be careful lest the light in you be darkness. (Luke 11:35 RSV)

It is not surprising that our *faults* cause us to appear flawed in God's eyes. But the fact that even our *virtues* are often only imperfections is what really ought to make us tremble.

Often our great spiritual wisdom is merely fleshly and worldly behavior. Our modesty is often only a composed—and hypocritical—outward appearance designed to observe social conventions and attract praise to ourselves. Our fervor can be just a mask for fierce moodiness or pride. Our frankness and openness with others can hide impatient brusqueness. And so on.

But in offering a sacrifice to God by making solemn promises to him, are we not promising to allow his dazzling light to show through us, as through the purest Christian virgin? But sometimes the sacrifice itself is executed with such great cowardliness that the light changes into darkness.

Therefore let us be careful lest the light within us be darkness.

forty-seven

The Blind World's Fate

Woe to the world for temptations to sin! (Matthew 18:7a, RSV)

Lord, let me be willing to repeat this awful saying by Jesus Christ, your Son and my Savior! These words are terrible for the world, which is forever rebuked, but they are sweet and comforting for those who love you and despise the world. For me these words would resound as terrifyingly as a clap of thunder if I ever turned my back on you and entered once again into slavery to this age.

Ah, blind world, what an unjust tyrant you are! You flatter so you can betray, you amuse and entertain so you can strike a death blow. You laugh and you entice men to laugh. But you despise people who weep; all you want to do is enchant the senses with a vain joy that turns into poison.

But you, vain world—you will weep forever, while God's children will be comforted. Oh, how I despise your contempt, and how afraid I am of falling into your complacency and self-satisfaction!

forty-eight

Love Not The World (1)

Do not love the world or the things in the world. (1 John 2:15 RSV)

How far-reaching these words of Jesus are! "The world" is the blind and corrupt multitude that Jesus Christ condemns in the gospel, and for whom he does not even pray as he is about to die.[21] All of us speak against the world—and yet each of us carries the world in our hearts.

"The world" is nothing other than all people who love themselves, and who love things without regard to God. Therefore, since all that men have to do to be classified as "the world" is to love themselves and to try to find in created things that which is only found in God, *we ourselves are the world.*

So let us own up to the fact that we belong to the world, and that we do not have the spirit of Jesus Christ. What a pity it is to give the outward appearance of renouncing the world, but all the while inwardly sustaining the world's thoughts and feelings!

[21] Cf. John 17:9.

forty-nine

Love Not The World (2)

But far be it for me to glory except in the cross of Jesus Christ, by which the world has been crucified to me, and I to the world. (Galatians 6:14 RSV)

When do we show that we love the world? When we are jealous of authority. When we love a reputation that we are not worthy of. When we spend idle time in the company of others. When we look for comforts that magnify the flesh. When we are weak and fainthearted in our Christian practices. When we do not take care to study the truths of the gospel.

So the world lives in us. But the truth is that we *desire* to live in it, since we so strongly desire for others to love us, and we are so afraid that others might forget us. How blessed and happy was Saint Paul, who was able to say, "The world has been crucified to me, and I to the world."

What a blessed thing it is to know how worthy of contempt the world is! It is making a very small sacrifice to God to sacrifice the world's fleeting illusions. How weak men are when they do not despise the world as it deserves! And how much men are to be pitied if they believe they have given up a great deal by taking leave of the world. Clergy, religious, or laymen seeking retirement from the world are only following that commitment more cautiously than the rest.

Indeed *all* of us Christians, through our baptism, have renounced the world. We are in search of the safe harbor if we turn and flee the raging storm.

fifty

Break My Bonds

I am not praying for the world but for those whom thou hast given me, for they are thine. (John 17:9b RSV)

As he was facing his life's end, Jesus Christ prayed for those who were about to torture him and put him to death—but he refused to pray for the world. So what should I think of those men who are known as decent and honest folk, and whom I have called my friends? Yet those who persecuted and murdered Jesus Christ were less hateful to him than those men to whom I once opened my heart in friendship.

What could I expect, seeing my weakness in the presence of those friends—men who take pride in forgetting God, in treating religious devotion as weakness, and in neglecting all their Christian duties? Can I really think that I love God and that I am not ashamed of his gospel, if I love the company of his enemies so much and am afraid of displeasing them by showing that I fear God?

O Lord! Bear me up against the swirling current of the world; break my bonds. Keep me far away from the tents of wickedness.[22] Join me in close union with those who love you.

[22] Psalm 84:10.

fifty-one

Dangerous Friends

Woe to the world for temptations to sin! *(Matthew 18:7a, RSV)*

The world already bears God's condemnation on its forehead, and yet it dares to set itself up as a judge to hand down decisions on every subject. We say we want to love God, and yet we cringe in fear of displeasing the world, God's irreconcilable enemy! O adulterous soul, unfaithful to the holy Bridegroom, do you not know that friendship with the world makes you an enemy of God? Therefore, woe to those who try to please the world—that blind, corrupt judge!

But what is "the world"? Is the world nothing but a mirage, an empty phrase? No! It is that crowd of worldly friends who carry on conversations with me every day, people who pass for moral folk, people who have their honor, people whom I love and by whom I am loved—but who do not love me for God's sake. Those are my most dangerous friends! An avowed enemy could only kill my body—but those people have killed my soul.

So that is what I mean by "the world"—and I must flee from it in horror, if my desire is to follow Jesus Christ.

fifty-two

On Fleeing From The World

But far be it from me to glory except in the cross of our Lord Jesus Christ, by which the world has been crucified to me, and I to the world. (Galatians 6:14 RSV)

We think we are far away from the world when we are in a place of quiet religious retreat. But we still speak the world's language; we have its feelings and curiosities. We still want a reputation and friendships. We want to be entertained. We still have high-minded opinions of ourselves. We still suffer the slightest humiliations with great indignation.

We *say* we want to forget the world, but in the depths of our hearts *we do not want to be forgotten by it*. We are searching to no avail when we try to find a halfway point between Jesus Christ and the world. As the apostle Paul said, it is not enough for the world to be dead to us. We must also be dead to it.

fifty-three

The Last Will Be First

And behold, some are last who will be first, and some are first who will be last. (Luke 13:30 RSV)

Many people live common, ordinary lives, but reach maturity in Christ. Yet many people who have taken vows to become Christ's chosen brides have been showered with God's graces and invited to taste the heavenly manna, but yet they languish in faintheartedness and immaturity!

Many sinners, who have spent years wandering far from God and paying no heed to the gospel, all at once turn away from their former life in earnest and fervent repentance. And often they surpass people who have tasted the gifts of the Holy Spirit from their earliest youth, and on whom God has granted his sweetest blessings! How beautiful it will be when those who are last win the garland of victory in this way, and by their example become the condemnation of those who were first!

But how painful it will be for those who were first when they become last, and find themselves behind people for whom they were once models. How painful it will be to lose their garlands, and to lose them for a few diversions that slowed them down!

I cannot help looking at the quiet, worshipful spirits of certain people who live in the world, and see how detached from the world and humble they are, without blushing with shame when I see how often we, who ought to be doing nothing but God's business, are dissolute, vain, and attached to our worldly goods.

So let us hasten to run, for fear of being left behind.

fifty-four

Attention To Love

Love one another earnestly from the heart. (1 Peter 1:22b
RSV)

Through these words the apostle Peter asks us to express
our love by always being careful not to hurt our neighbor.
Without careful attention, love—which is so fragile in this
life—is quickly lost. One word said curtly or irritably or
with a haughty or disdainful look, can affect those who are
weak.

We need to take great care with others, as they are so dear
to God and are such precious members of the body of Jesus
Christ. If you are lacking in this care, then you are also lacking in love—because we cannot love without giving our
attention to the object of our love. This attention to love

ought to fill our whole beings—our minds and our hearts.

It seems to me that I hear Jesus Christ saying to you, as he said to Saint Peter, "If you love Me, feed my sheep."[23]

---

[23] John 21:17.

fifty-five

Service To Others

For the Son of man also came not to be served but to serve. (Mark 10:45a RSV)

Jesus Christ came not to be served, but to serve. And this is what everyone who has any authority over other people ought to be saying; this is what pure ministry is. Those whom we appear to command, we should in reality be serving. We must suffer their imperfections, lift them up gently and patiently when they fall, and wait for them to follow along God's path. We must become all things to everyone and think of ourselves as having been made for them.

We need to humble ourselves in order to gently speak the most needed corrections. We must never give up in discouragement. Instead, we need to ask God to change their heart—something we cannot do ourselves.

So examine yourself with respect to the people who have been given to you to care for, and for whom you bear responsibility in the sight of God.

fifty-six

A Humble Heart

Learn of me; for I am meek and lowly in heart. (from Matthew 11:29 KJV)

The Son of God was the only one who could teach us this divine lesson. As Saint Paul told us, Jesus is the One who "always had the nature of God, but he did not think that by force he should try to become equal with God."[24] What has he not done out of love for us? What has he not suffered at our hands, and what does he suffer still? As Isaiah said, "Like a lamb about to be slaughtered, like a sheep about to be sheared, he never said a word [of complaint]."[25]

But look at us—we grumble about the smallest problems; we are vain, fragile, and overly sensitive. There is no true or constant gentleness without humility. As long as we are full of ourselves, everything in us will be shocked by faults in other people.

If we are convinced that nothing is our rightful due, then *nothing will make us bitter.* If we think often of how destitute we are, we will become merciful toward weaknesses in other people.

As Saint Augustine tells us, there is not a single page in the Scriptures where God does not thunder forth these great and loving words, "Learn of me; for I am meek and lowly in heart."

[24] Philippians 2:6-7, TEV.
[25] Isaiah 53:7, TEV.

fifty-seven

True Glory

For everyone who exalts himself will be humbled, and he who humbles himself will be exalted. (Luke 14:11 RSV)

Since we so love a lofty place, let us seek loftiness where it can be found: let us look for the high place that will last forever. What an admirable ambition—to want to reign for all ages with the Son of God and to be seated forever on the same throne with him!

But such ambition it is—such childish jealousy—to be eager to have a name among men! If we do so we will achieve a reputation that is even less solid than smoke that turns into the plaything of the wind! Is it worth all the trouble we put ourselves through to have a few people say they are our friends without really being so, and to keep up vain appearances?

Let us aspire to real greatness. True greatness can be found only by making ourselves humble here on earth. God opposes proud people, starting in this life. He brings envy, criticism and slander on them and causes them to suffer untold setbacks. And finally he will humble them in eternity.

But one who is humble, who remains hidden, who desires to be forgotten, and is afraid of being sought out by the world, will *already in this life* be respected for not wanting to be sought out. And eternal glory will be the reward for his disregard for false and contemptible glory.

fifty-eight

Our Deliverer Is Coming

Rejoice in the Lord always; again I will say, Rejoice. Let all men know your forbearance. The Lord is at hand. (Philippians 4:4-5 RSV)

Our distaste for our uncontrolled emotions and for the world's hollow vanities ought to be the spring from which our joy flows. The only foundation of our joy should be our hope, and we can hope only to the extent that we are dissatisfied with the world.

Our anticipation of Jesus' coming ought to make us modest, self-disciplined and faithful. One day he will come and give us a garland of honor—and we need to hold ourselves at the ready to receive him. We should be glad that he is coming, because although he will be the world's Judge, he will be our comforter.

It is so sweet to be at peace, waiting expectantly for Jesus Christ, while the children of this age are afraid of his appearing! They will tremble and shudder. And we? We will see our beloved rescuer coming. What a happy, enviable state to be in!

So you have not yet reached that state? Then aspire to it! The only things that keep us from being in that state of trust and consolation are our faintheartedness and our desire for pleasure.

fifty-nine

The Flesh And The Word

He who eats me will live because of me. (John 6:57b RSV)

We eat the body of Jesus Christ, but his Spirit is what gives us life. As he himself said, the flesh is of no avail.[26] The flesh is united to the Word in such a way that Saint John was not afraid to say, "the Word became flesh."[27]

Yet God joined the flesh and the Word for the sole purpose of communicating his Spirit to us in a way that we are better able to touch and feel. By so doing he reaches down and becomes one with us in the flesh. He gives us his flesh to eat only to make us one body with him, and to bring our souls to life with his divine life.

So why is it that we, who so often obtain life *from* him, refuse to live *for* him? What becomes of that bread from heaven, that wholly divine flesh? What purpose does our receiving communion serve? Does Jesus Christ live inside us? Do his thoughts and actions show forth in our human flesh? Are we growing in Jesus Christ because of our feeding on him?

How shameful it is that we are always searching for pleasure, always grumbling at the slightest suffering, always crawling around searching for comfort in the most miserable of places, always hiding our faults without correcting them—while at the same time we have been joined into one flesh with Jesus Christ himself!

[26] John 6:63.
[27] John 1:14.

sixty

Christ Lives—In Me

He who eats me will live because of me. (John 6:57b RSV)
It is no longer I who live, but Christ who lives in me.
(from Galatians 2:20 RSV)

Jesus Christ is our whole life—that is the eternal truth that
ought to nourish, teach and sustain us. So why is it that we
can feed on such a divine source of nourishment and yet continue to waste away? How can we fail to grow in virtue,
resist growing in spiritual health and strength, live in false-
hood, harbor dangerous desires in our hearts, and fail to
take pleasure in the only source of true good? Is that the life
of a Christian who eats the bread from Heaven?

Jesus Christ wants only to unite himself with us and join
with us in body and in spirit. Why? So he can live deep with-

in our hearts. He must be manifested in our mortal bodies; he must radiate from us, since he and we have become one flesh. I live, yet "it is no longer I who live, but Christ who lives in me"—his created child who has died already to the things of the world.

sixty-one

Rest In God's Heart

I slept, but my heart was awake. (Song of Solomon 5:2 RSV)

Our sleep will be peaceful when we rest in God's heart, abandoning ourselves to his providence and ever maintaining a sweet awareness of his mercy. When we do this, we are no longer seeking anything for ourselves, and our entire being rests in him.

What we leave behind are our faltering and troubled rationalizations, our desires for ourselves, our impatience to gain a higher place. Then we find ourselves resting in the heart of God[28]—for God is the one who has put us there with his own hands, and he cradles us there in his arms.

Can we be in danger where God places us—a place where we are as a little child who is rocked and hugged by its mother? Let us let go and give him the freedom to act. Let us rest on him and in him.

This confident, trusting rest, which quells every movement of our limited human reasoning, comes as we maintain true vigilance over our hearts. To place ourselves in God's hands without leaning on any person or any thing—this is what it is to keep our hearts awake even as we sleep.

In this way love will always jealously keep its eyes open; it will always reach out to its Beloved. And when we do that, we will not fall into the deadly sleep of our souls.

[28] *Le sein de Dieu*: the heart, the bosom, the womb. (Further explanation is given in this volume's foreword.)

sixty-two

Teach Us To Pray

Lord, teach us to pray. *(Luke 11:1 RSV)*

Lord, I do not know what I ought to be asking of you. You are the only One who knows what I need. You love me better than I know how to love myself. O Father!—give your child what I do not know how to ask for myself. I do not dare ask for crosses or for consolation. All I can do is present myself to you.

Lord, I open up my heart to you. Behold my needs—the ones that I am not even aware of. Look at them, and act according to your mercy. Bring suffering on me or heal me, cast me down or raise me up—I adore your will for me even when I do not know what it is.

I will remain silent, offering myself up and giving myself

over completely to you. I no longer have any desire other than to accomplish your will. Teach me to pray; may you yourself pray in me and through me.

sixty-three

Where Is Our Love?

Lord, you know everything; you know that I love you.
(Saint Peter, in John 21:17 RSV)

Do we dare to say this to our Lord as Saint Peter did? Are we loving God even when we are not thinking about him? What friend is there with whom we would like to speak if not with him? Where do we become more bored and restless than in church?

What are we doing to please our Master and to make ourselves as he wants us to be? What are we doing for his glory? What have we sacrificed for him in order to accomplish his will? Do we prefer his will over our slightest interests, over our smallest sources of pleasure? Where is that love we think we have?

Saint Paul warned: "If anyone has no love for the Lord, let him be accursed."[29] Woe to him who does not love the Lord Jesus, who has loved us so much. Will he give his eternal kingdom to those who do not love him? If we loved him, could we be unresponsive to his blessings, to his inspirations, to his graces?

"For I am persuaded that neither death, nor life, nor angels, nor principalities, nor powers, nor things present, nor things to come, nor height, nor depth, nor any other creature, shall be able to separate us from the love of God, which is in Christ Jesus, our Lord."[30]

[29] 1 Corinthians 16:22, RSV.
[30] Romans 8:38-39, KJV.

sixty-four

Behold My Love

"Yes, Lord; you know that I love you." *(Saint Peter, in*
John 21:15 RSV)

O dear God, O dear Father, O my all in all, you know better than I do how much I love you. You know it, but I do not
know it myself—because nothing is more hidden to me than
the depths of my heart.

I want to love you. I am afraid of not loving you enough.
What I am asking you for is an abundance of pure love. You
see my desire—and indeed you are the one who is creating it
within me. So look inside the heart of this mortal that you
have created, and behold the love you have placed within me.

O God, you who love me enough to inspire me to love you
to the utmost, please do not look any longer on the torrent

of unconfessed sin that once engulfed me. Look within me and see only your mercy—and my love.

sixty-five

Seek First God's Kingdom

But seek first his kingdom and his righteousness, and all these things shall be yours as well. (Jesus, in Matthew 6:33 RSV)

Are we not ashamed to seek something from God? We have the very source of every good thing, yet we think we are still poor.

Even in their religious devotion some seek a source of worldly comfort and consolation. They look at religious devotion as a way to lighten the pains they are suffering and not as a state of turning away from themselves and making sacrifices. That mistake is the source of every discouragement.

Let us begin by placing ourselves in God's hands. As we serve him, let us never become anxious and troubled about what he will do for us.

Life is so short—if we suffer a little less or a little more, that is no great thing, when we keep our sight on the kingdom that will last forever.

sixty-six

I Shall Not Want

The Lord is my shepherd; I shall not want. *(Psalm 23:1 KJV)*

When I have God, what else could I want? Truly, God himself is the only good there is—and his goodness is never-ending. And so I say to all the falsely "good" things of the earth, "Get away from me! You are unworthy of bearing the name 'good.' The only thing you are good for is to make men bad!" Nothing is good except God. He is in my heart, and I will always carry him within me.

It does not matter if God takes away my pleasures, my riches, my honors, my authority, my friends, my health, and even my life. As long as he does not hide himself from my heart, I will always be rich; I will not have lost anything at all. No, I will have held onto the One who is of everything.

The Lord has been searching for me in all my wanderings away from him. He has loved me when I have not loved him. He has looked on me with gentle tenderness in spite of my ingratitude. I am in his hands. He is leading me according to his wishes.

I feel how weak I am—and how strong God is. And if I keep my trust in his power, I will never lack for anything.

sixty-seven

Hunger For God

Whom have I in heaven but thee? And having thee, I desire nothing else on earth. Though heart and body fail, yet God is my possession for ever. (Psalm 73:25-26 NEB)

Lord, you are the God of all nature, and everything obeys your voice. You are the soul of every living thing and even of every non-living thing. You are my soul even more than this very soul that you gave to my body. You are closer to me than myself. All things belong to you; should my heart not also belong to you—this heart that you made and to which you give life? It is yours, not mine.

But you, O dear God, you also belong to me, because I love you. You are everything for me. I have no other possession, O my eternal inheritance! What I long for is not earthly

consolations, pleasant feelings inside, brilliant enlightenment, or even extraordinary inner graces. I am not asking for
any of those gifts that come from you but which are still not
you yourself.

I hunger and thirst for you and you alone. I want to forget myself, to lose sight of myself. Do with me according to
your will. Nothing else matters. I love you.

sixty-eight

Unshakable Desire For God

Glory to God in the highest, and on earth peace, good will toward men. (Luke 2:14 KJV)

When we seek only the glory of God, we will find our peace again. But God's glory is not to be found in all the thoughts and actions of man. God wants to be glorified only through our bringing our human nature down to nothing and giving ourselves completely over to his Spirit. We must not want his glory more than he wants it himself. So let us give ourselves over as quiet instruments for carrying out his divine plan.

Many things will have to be rooted out: our bustling urgency, our movements based on self, our restless agitation that comes disguised as zeal. When these are gone—that is true peace and good will.

The way to have a good will that conforms to God's is to give up our desires and fears and to leave ourselves completely in his hands. Those who do so are as unshakable as Mount Zion.[31] They can never be moved, because their only desire is for God. And it is God who brings everything to pass.

---

[31] "Those who trust in the Lord are like Mount Zion, which cannot be moved, but abides for ever." (Psalm 125:1, RSV)

sixty-nine

Learning From The Master (1)

Learn from me; for I am gentle and lowly in heart, and you will find rest for your souls. (Matthew 11:29b rsv)

O God, I am coming to sit at your feet to be taught and examined by you. You are present here; you are drawing me here by your grace. I am listening only to you. I believe only in you.

Lord, I worship you. My heart loves only you. It longs for you alone. It is with joy that I bring myself low before you, O eternal Majesty. I come to receive everything from your hand, and to renounce myself without reservation.

O God, send your Holy Spirit. Let your Spirit become mine, and let my own mind and spirit be forever brought to nothing! I give myself over to that Spirit of love and truth.

137

Let him illumine me today and teach me to be gentle and lowly in heart!

O Jesus, you are the One who is teaching me this lesson in gentleness and lowliness. Anyone else who might want to teach it to me would only repel me; everywhere I would see only imperfection and pride. So you are the One who must teach me.

Speak, Lord, for your servant is listening.

seventy

Learning From The Master (2)

[Jesus] taught them as one who had authority. (from Matthew 7:29 RSV)

Good teacher, you reach down to teach me through your example. What authority! All I have to do is to fall silent, to worship, to merge myself with you, to pattern myself after you.

The Son of God came down from heaven to dwell among mortals, took on a body made of dust, and died on the cross. All this to make me deeply ashamed of my pride. The One who was everything brought himself down to nothing. And I who am nothing, I want to be—or at least I want people to believe me to be—everything that am not. Such lies! Such foolishness! Such impudent vanity! Such devilish presumption!

What kind of person could claim to be excused from following your example? Could the lowliest person? Could the sinner who has so often shown such terrible ingratitude that he or she is worthy only to be struck down by your justice?

But Lord, you did not just tell me, "Be gentle and humble." No, you said that *you* are gentle and humble. It is enough to know that this is who you are to conclude that we want to be like you.

seventy-one

Learning From The Master (3)

Learn from me; for I am gentle and lowly in heart, and you will find rest for your souls. (Matthew 11:29b RSV)

Dear God, you are both *gentle* and *lowly*, because lowliness—humility—is the source of true gentleness. Pride is always haughty, impatient, ready to become bitter. But people who in good faith make light of themselves are willing to be made light of by others. People who believe that nothing is owed to them never believe they are being mistreated.

Acting according to our nature, we cannot produce true-gentleness. We can only produce lifelessness, indifference, or artful deception. To be gentle toward another person, we have to let go of ourselves.

And then, dear Lord, you add, ". . . gentle and lowly *in heart.*" Lowliness is not putting ourselves down only in our minds; humility comes through a heartfelt desire—our wills consent to it and grow to love it so we may glorify God. It comes through taking pleasure in seeing our wretched condition, bringing ourselves low before God, so that we may owe our healing to him alone. Merely to see how wretched we are and to fall into despair over what we see is not being humble. On the contrary, to do that is to have a fit of pride that cannot consent to being brought low.

Finally, dear Savior, you promise me that in humility I will find rest for my soul. Alas! How far astray I have gone from that kind of peace! I have searched for it in foolish and turbulent passions, and in the vain imaginations of my pride. But pride cannot coexist with peace. Pride always wants what it cannot have; it always wants to pass itself off as something it is not. It constantly rears its head, and constantly God resists it. He brings our pride low through the envy or contradiction of other people or through our own faults that we cannot help being aware of.

Cursed pride, you will never enjoy the peace of God's children who are simple and small in their own eyes!

seventy-two

Make Me Worthy

Dear God, how good you are to make me love your peace![32] But it is not enough for me to love and desire it. Make me worthy of it—by crushing my pride. Bring down my mind as well as my body. Let my pride be able to breathe no longer. Complete the work you have begun in taking me out of worldly fellowship with those who neither know you nor love you. Quench in me even the last vestiges of my fierce shame. Break the bonds that keep me a prisoner, and forge new ones that attach me to you alone.

What have I done to you, dear God, to be worthy of such undeserved mercy! The grace you showed me in the past, I trampled under foot. I have repaid with ingratitude all your former goodness toward me. So the only merit that I have in your sight is this: *I am in such a wretched condition that you are moved to show mercy.*

Knowing that, will I still hesitate between the world, which wants me to be lost, and you, who want to save me? Will I push away the cross you offer me with such love, to deliver me from the sickness of my soul—a sickness more terrible than illnesses of the body?

O Lord, I throw myself on your mercy. I am worthy only to be handed over to your eternal justice. Chasten me, Lord, chasten me. Do with me according to your good pleasure. I want no other will than yours. I will praise you in all my sufferings. I will kiss the hand that chastens me. I believe that I will yet be spared.

Lord, I stand ready for anything you send me—whether that means living separated from the world, confessing aloud the good news of your gospel, or dying on the cross with you. O Jesus, you are my love and my life.

[32] "Therefore love truth and peace." (Zechariah 8:19b RSV)

seventy-three

See God's Mercy[33]

*I will keep quiet, I will not say a word, for you are the
One who made me suffer like this.* (Psalm 39:9 TEV)

Is it my place to complain when God afflicts me, knowing
that it is out of love that he makes me suffer in order to heal
me? Therefore, Lord, correct me—I give you my permission.

And yet, how gentle are your hardest blows, since they
hide such mercy! Alas! If you had not afflicted my body, my
soul would never have stopped administering its own death
blow. It was covered with the most horrible sores. You saw
my soul, you had mercy on it. Now you are bringing down
this body full of sin. You are reversing my ambitious plans.
You are giving me back the desire for your eternal truth,
which I had lost so long ago.

Dear Lord, may you be forever blessed! I bend over to kiss the hand that is correcting me. I worship the arm that is reaching out to chastise me.

[33] This meditation and those that follow are taken from *Meditations For One Who Is Ill*. They are the cry of the heart to God in a time of physical and emotional suffering.

seventy-four

Life-Giving Pain

Be merciful to me, O Lord, for I am weak. (Psalm 6:2a
NEB)

Dear God, I cannot offer anything that could cause you to
have mercy on me—except my unworthiness. Look and see
how much I need your help, and reach out to help me. I am
aware of my need. And Lord, I am happy to be aware of it,
if that awareness helps me keep mistrusting myself! You
have afflicted my flesh in order to purify it. You have broken
my body to heal my soul. With life-giving pain, you are tearing me away from corrupt pleasures.

My physical suffering afflicts me deeply. Yet I was blithely
untroubled by the illness of my soul, which had fallen prey
to vain ambition, to the burning fever of raging passions. I

was sick, and I did not believe I was. My sickness was so great that I was not even aware of it. I was like a man with a high fever who mistakes the burning of his fever for the flush of good health. How blessed is my sickness, because it is opening my eyes and changing my heart!

seventy-five

The Precious Gift Of Suffering

For it has been granted to you that for the sake of Christ you should not only believe in him but also suffer for his sake. (Philippians 1:29 RSV)

What a precious gift suffering is, and we do not recognize it! Suffering is no less precious than the faith poured out in our souls by the Holy Spirit. It is a blessed sign of mercy when God makes us suffer!

But is our suffering to be forced and full of impatience? No, that is the way the demons suffer. One who suffers without being willing to suffer will find in his affliction the mere beginning of eternal sorrow. Whoever submits to God in his suffering transforms his anguish into infinite good.

Therefore, dear God, I long to suffer in peace and with love. It is not enough to believe your holy truths—we must follow them. They condemn us to suffering, but they reveal its value.

Lord, bring new life to my languishing faith. Let others see the faith and patience of your saints shining once again in me! And if some impatient word escapes my lips, at least let me immediately humble myself and offer reparation for it through my suffering!

seventy-six

Sustain My Heart

O Lord, I am oppressed; be thou my security! (Hezekiah, in Isaiah 38:14 RSV)

You see all these painful things that are afflicting me. My body is complaining—what shall I reply to it? The world is trying to gain my attention and flatter me; how must I push it away? What shall I say, Lord? Alas, I have only enough strength to suffer and remain silent.

Answer me yourself through your almighty Word. Thrust aside the deceitful world that has already seduced me once. Sustain my heart, despite the weakness of my nature. I am suffering intensely because of the troubles with which you are afflicting me, and because of my strong passions that have not yet been extinguished.

Lord, I am suffering—come quickly to help me! Deliver me from the world and from myself. Deliver me from my troubles by giving me the patience to suffer them.

seventy-seven

Give Me Yourself

The Lord gave, and the Lord has taken away. (from Job 1:21 RSV)

Lord, these are the words you gave your servant Job to say as his troubles multiplied. How good you are to once again put those words in the mouth and in the heart of such a sinner as I! You once gave me health, and I forgot you; you have taken it away, and now I am coming back to you. O precious mercy, you are wrenching away God's gifts that were separating me from him, in order to give me God himself!

Lord, take away anything in me that is not you, provided only that you give me yourself. Everything belongs to you. You are the Lord. Take charge of everything—worldly

goods, honors, health, life. Tear away—down to the roots—
everything that would take your place within me.

seventy-eight

Be My Patience

Come unto me, all ye that labor and are heavy laden, and I will give you rest. *(Matthew 11:28 RSV)*

What a sweet and gentle word this is from Jesus Christ, who takes on himself all the burdens, all the weariness, and all the sufferings of mankind! Dearest Savior, do you truly want to carry all my troubles? Yes, you are inviting me to lay them on your shoulders. All that I suffer is meant to find relief in you.

So, Lord, I join my cross to yours. Carry it for me. I am falling down in exhaustion—just as you once were when another person was made to carry your cross. Lord, I am walking after you toward Calvary, to be crucified there. And when it is your will, I want to die in your arms.

But the weight of my cross is crushing me. I do not have enough patience—be my patience yourself. I beg of you to do as you have promised. I am coming to you; I cannot go on any more.

And this is enough to be worthy of your compassion and your help.

seventy-nine

Your Servant Is Listening

Speak, Lord, your servant is listening. (1 Samuel 3:9, TEV)

Lord, I am keeping silent in my affliction. I am keeping silent, but I am listening to you with the silence of a contrite, humble soul to whom there is nothing left to say in its suffering.

Dear God, you see my wounds. You are the One who made them. You are the One who is bringing them on me. I am keeping silent. I am suffering. And I am adoring you in the midst of my silence. But you hear my sighs of grief, and the groans of my heart are not hidden from you.

Lord, I do not want to listen to myself. All I want to do is listen to you and follow you.

eighty

Deliver Me From Myself

Father, save me from this hour. (from John 12:27 KJV)

Dear God, even though you are placing me in peril and afflicting me, you are my Father, and you always will be. Deliver me from this terrible hour I am going through, this time of bitterness and despondency!

Let me breathe on your breast and die in your arms. Save me—either by diminishing my troubles or by increasing my patience. Cut to the quick, burn the chaff. But have mercy, take pity on my weakness.

And if it is not your will to deliver me from my suffering, then deliver me from myself, from my weakness, from my sensitiveness, from my impatience.

eighty-one

Flooded With Grace

Against thee, thee only, have I sinned. (Psalm 51:4 RSV)

I have sinned against all your laws. In my pride, my slackness and my bad example, there is nothing holy in religion that I have not violated. I have even caused offense against your Holy Spirit. I have trampled on the blood of the covenant. I have rejected the former mercies that once penetrated my heart. Lord, I have done every evil thing.

I have exhausted every iniquity, but I have not exhausted your mercy. On the contrary, your mercy takes pleasure in overcoming my unworthiness. It rises like a flood over a dike. In return for so much evil, you give me back everything good. And since you are giving yourself, dear God, to one who has sinned so much, and you are flooding me with grace, shall I refuse to carry my cross along with your Son, who is righteousness and holiness itself?

eighty-two

My Strength Fails Me

My strength fails me. (from Psalm 38:10 RSV)

My strength fails me. I feel nothing but weakness, impatience, the affliction of a feeble nature, and the temptation to murmur and despair. What has become of the courage of which I was so proud, and which inspired in me so much confidence in myself? Alas! Besides all my troubles, I also have to endure the shame of my weakness and my impatience.

Lord, you are attacking my pride on every side; you are leaving it no resources at all. I am all too happy to endure these things, provided that through these terrible lessons you teach me that I am nothing, that I am capable of nothing, and that you alone are everything!

eighty-three

Join Me To Yourself

And I, when I am lifted up from the earth, will draw all men to myself. (John 12:32 RSV)

Lord, you promised that when you were lifted up on the cross, you would draw all men to yourself. The nations have come to worship the Man of sorrows. Jews in great numbers have recognized the crucified One as Savior. So your promise has indeed been carried out in the sight of the whole world. But from high up on your cross your almighty power and virtue continue to draw souls to you.

O suffering God! You are taking me out of the deceitful world. You are tearing me away from myself and my vain desires, so that you may cause me to suffer with you on the cross.

It is on the cross that we belong to you; it is on the cross that we come to know you; it is on the cross that we love you; it is on the cross that we are fed with your truth. Without the cross, everything else is nothing but religious sentimentalism. Jesus, join me to yourself! Let me become one of the members of the body of the crucified Jesus Christ!

eighty-four

Set Me Free

Woe to the world for temptations to sin! (Matthew 18:6 RSV)

The world says, "How terrible for those who suffer!" But from the depths of my heart faith replies, "How terrible for the world when it does *not* suffer!" The world sows the entire earth with evil traps to cause souls to go astray. For a long time my own soul was lost in the world. Alas!

Dear God, how good you are to use my infirmity to hold me far away from that corrupt world.

Strengthen me through suffering and complete your work of setting me free from everything, before you allow me to become exposed to those enemies of yours who tempt to sin. Let my infirmity teach me to know that the world's delights are full of poison.

eighty-five

The Sacrifice Of My Days

Whether we live or whether we die, we are the Lord's.
(Romans 14:8 RSV)

Dear God, what does it matter to me whether I live or die?
Life is nothing. It is even dangerous once we start loving it.
All death can do is destroy a body made of clay. But it delivers
the soul from sickness of the body and from its own pride.
Death takes the soul away from the devil's traps and makes
it pass for all eternity into the kingdom of truth.

Therefore, dear God, I am not asking you for health or
life. I am offering you a sacrifice of my days. You have num-
bered them; I am not asking for any extension of them. What
I *am* asking is to die rather than to live as I have lived. If you
want me to die, I will die in patience and love.

O God, you hold in your hands the keys of the grave; you can open it or shut it. Do not give me life, if I cannot become detached from it. But whether I live or whether I die, from this moment on I want to be entirely yours.